# FIRST THIRTY

Margaret Chideme

First published 2023
by Rowanvale Books Ltd
The Gate
Keppoch Street
Roath
Cardiff
CF24 3JW
www.rowanvalebooks.com

A CIP catalogue record for this book is available from the British Library.
ISBN: 978-1-914422-67-6
Hardback ISBN: 978-1-914422-68-3
ePub ISBN: 978-1-914422-66-9

# Acknowledgments

**Charles Mungoshi Jr** (The Hub of Positivity) – Thank you for your guidance and support, for showing me the ropes and which direction to take in my new endeavor. Thank you for walking the walk with me. There is no editor more passionate than you. I am forever grateful.

**Dominic Mereki** (Stitch Studios) – You and your beautiful wife understood my vision from the first time I met you, and you believed in my work. I knew I'd come to the right place because you felt like a kindred spirit. Thank you for your beautiful artistry and interpretation of my work. You took your time and made sure you were aligned with my words. You are appreciated greatly.

**Tafadzwa Taruvinga**, author of *The Educated Waiter: Memoir of an African Immigrant* – For the advice and words of wisdom you gave me as a fellow writer, thank you.

**Tafadzwa Chinhengo** – You have been the keeper of my work for so many years, an editor, my cheerleader, my free consultant and most trusted friend. I appreciate you, pumpkin.

**Mr Chigariro** – I'm sure you had no idea how much your literature lessons ignited my love story with words. I will forever cherish you, my favorite teacher of all time.

**Mom, Daphne and Nigel** – Thank you for always allowing me to be me. Thank you for supporting me in my dreams. Thank you for loving me.

**GR** – For your ideas, advice, inspiration, unwavering support and love.


**Ava** – You are the reason I do it all.


**Shingirirai Mavima**, author of *Pashena: The Dirt Field* and the anthologies *Homeward Bound* and *Mirage of Days Old* – Thank you for your advice when the book was still just an idea. Your encouragement and practical steps propelled me to action.

To her…

# Table of Contents

# Her pain…The tears

*For to love is to live and to hurt is to feel…*

*Her pain... The tears*

# Silent Cries

Female...Black

African, Female...aaaannnd Black

3 minority qualities rolled into one...

With wings clutched...

Born with an illusion to fly

Why are you so daring...? Shut up!!!

Think you are a man?

"Real women walk with their heads bowed down"

African, Female and Black...

So much more to hide

Inner stride bold…

Outer crawl cold…

Audacious…admired usually?

Rather…audacious…deserving of a smacking to put you "right"

Fate in those who "own" you

Their rights earned by a last name...

...By birth or by a couple of thousands or cows paid

A misstep...a mishap...a mistake...?

Who cares...?

Reality is...it's there

Never fully equally human as a man

African...Female and Black...born a slave

Never mind the seeming curse…

The Silent Cries…

There is royalty to that name…

Royalty to the purpose

"African…Female and Black"

"Daring and audacious…"

Could be qualities of greatness instead…

## Hail Oh Female Black African Queen...

Remind them...

...Remind yourself of your price

.........Priceless.........

Never believe otherwise

*...Silent Cries*

# As I lie next to you

It all comes back to me as I lie next to you

That the arm tightly holding me is the same that blackened and bruised my thigh...my cheek, the other time

*As I lie next to you*

It all comes back to me as I lie next to you

That those lips that love to suckle my breast are the same that speak words that chip at my chest...

It all comes back to me as I lie next to you

The same body you caress is the same body you have come to loathe…disrespect in the most unimaginable ways…

My God-given soul's canvas…my home has become your playground…

No longer your sacred half but rather scared half…is this my life now? Till what do us apart?

It all comes back to me as I lie next to you

That I have become a shell so hollow and I've let your song play and my melody fade...gone...gone...

Now less of a human but mere property to pain...

For the victim is no different than the perpetrator...all buried in a web of unconscious fear of change

It all comes back to me as I lie next to you

That another day in the same bed makes it a choice to stay

And for some...for me...this could be the very last breath that I take

It all comes back to me as I lie next to you...

*...As I lie next to you*

# Nhlanhla

Nhlanhla your ego is poison...grabbing my body like I owe you something

Nhlanhla you strut like a peacock entitled with that "little cock"

Nhlanhla your tales tell of a horror story

Plastering your songs of fear on me so that I don't tell my story

Nhlanhla you vile pig

Forcing yourself on me like a tick

Locking that door and tearing my stockings

Nhlanhla...Nhlanhla you stole from me and in silence I weep

But the dress I wore I will still keep

For the love for it beams still

You took a part of me, and that I can't erase

But my soul is mine to keep

And watch your back; I'm coming for you still

Filthy Nhlanhla you son of a bitch

...Nhlanhla

# Life's filled fury

Dices of heartbreak nicely chopped

Cups of deliciously marinated life-destroying gossip

Would you dare add a pinch of devil's slap?

Then top it off with strings of financial dismay

Drop in my smooth path mountains of sharp piercing thorns

Iced with kisses of hate-filled venom

Make me a nice bowl of life's filled fury

Come on I dare you, is this all you have got?

Look here, let me face you

The horror on your face as I rise above it all...

*...Life's filled fury*

# Guarded heart

*She* was taught to love is to hurt…To hurt is to love

Her guarded heart only partly lover…

Yielding again completely…? Never!!! Would she, she vowed…

Maybe…only partly to another

A suitor once exposed her to herself as unyielding...

Beautiful and untamable he chanted dreamingly...

Although she seems seemingly taken...

Possibly enchanted he said...

But realistically she's odd...probably almost cold

Repetitive cycles taught her a lesson too obvious...

Passion, jealously, all signs of uncontrollable desire in lovers

She's exhausted...

Her guarded heart...heart scared to discover...

True love incessantly demanding...

What if her fears are on point...romance perfectly surreal

Vulnerable in love...and the kiss of romance equals a kiss from the serpent

Paralyzing fear swallows all of love's space

True love demanding her heart...a brave heart indeed

But truly if love lives for all eternity

Her guarded heart should spit her poison...

For to love is to live and to hurt is to feel

*...Guarded heart*

# Last Night

Last night I had a dream

I dreamt of a man with a face I could not recognize

But my heart knew who he was

He looked at me with eyes I could not see

But his gaze I could feel inside

His arms held me so close

He kissed me and took my breath away

An emotion arose in me that was unknown

It moved me and made my whole body explode

I held him for as long as I could dream

Because I knew he would be gone when I awoke

Last night I had a dream

I dreamt of the man of my dreams

And only there he exists

...Last Night

# 60 seconds

*Can* I find poetry in the sound of pain?

With the intent of happiness, conviction and fulfillment?

You are seeping through my being, each lingering thought of you

Fragments of past hurt, past love, past tense?

As if it's a healing wound still exposed

Things I should have done differently?

Ways in which I could have understood you better?

Could you have loved me better?

Instead, we had the name-calling and the finger-pointing

Emotional, mental, physical torture

Abuse...

You could have killed me

Instead of cheating...

...Was I fleeing?

The love undeniably present...

If love was enough we could have survived it

But is it ever? Really?

One man's survival is another man's poison

We spoke too differently

...Felt feelings apart for us to unite

As I lie on my bed tonight

Gazing at the imagined calming moon and stars

Ribbons of possibility...Options

...Ideas flying down exposed for me to see

...The truth is revealed...

I've got to let you go

What I write is about you

Most of what I want is you

Yet all of what I am scared of, is you...

I cry tears, streaming down like rivers, sounding water...

What should have been? I don't know

I just know that I cannot do this anymore

but just give me 60 more seconds to mourn us

To moan you

Our dying love

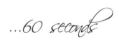

...60 seconds

# Broken Vows

*I*magined happily ever after...

Vaporized as the moments pass

The cold nights alone...

The unanswered calls...

Faded until dawn...

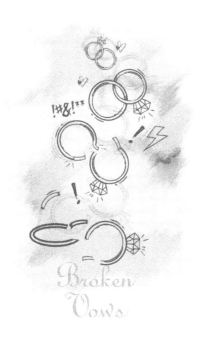

The dishonest eyes that face the disappointed face

The lips that lied the time away

The broken promises that invaded the vows

And the fear of loss that consumed the house

Depressed souls scattered and shattered cowardly so

Feelings of insecurity clouded any potential future so

Home built on sand, foundation with creaking sounds

Broken Vows, Broken dreams

They all sing a song of melancholic bliss...

# You, Lisa and I

The scent of your skin sets my heart pulsating

The touch of your strong, masculine hand grazes my face

I feel your influence caress my body

Sending my blood into a flow of gushing delight


My heartbeat increases into a fast rhythmic pace

Your lips touch mine...lightly...so soft

In response...searching inside the passion I see mirrored in your eyes

Intoxicating my mind into thoughts of ecstasy

Just so infinitely, intimately divine


You pull me close; your lips whisper something in my ear

My eyes lightly closed, I feel myself floating into a different world

Your hand grips my succulence and closer you pull me to you

You whisper yet something again in my ear

I open my eyes abruptly as I realize what you just said

"Lisa?!!!!" But that's not my name!!!!!

...*You, Lisa and I*

# But so on…go on

*Forgot* to breathe as you spoke

Soaked up your words like a smitten sponge

I'm left wanting more…

Feels like I'm gasping for more…each time we are alone

I slow the moment down

...Down to the slow sensual meeting of your lips as you speak

When you were telling me that dumb story...

The one that started the first time you saw me...

...You know it

My body sinks beneath yours

My mind contoured and intrigued by yours

You are drawing me in...

Into the kind of submission I'd vowed never to know

I hear you tell me…

I see you see me…

I kinda feel you grounded…

But I can't seem to touch your invisible toes

It's a long walk between us understanding our different thoughts...

Our different stories and wars...

Can't get past the distant trails of stolen time...

Past the wails and walls of disappointment in love

When can we trust that it's real?

When you both love and hate me at the same time

And I do too sometimes...

Karmic poetic justice in roles reversed this time

I miss my friend...

You punished me and took him away

He would always come and go like the lover did

As the seasons passed...as time eased

It was very easy and carefree

With no worry of the illusion of chasing time

I miss my friend...like a lover he'd soothe

...All my worldly worries away in meaningless careless laughter we cooed

Now I'm caught between lover, friend and foe

I despise this enemy who leaves my heart exposed, sore and raw

With deafening silent screams in the loss of control I can't seem to stop

This enemy doesn't seem to like to talk...

...By the way

I did want to kiss you that day

Then maybe slap you a moment after...

After savoring the different flavors from the passion of your bottled-up pit

Blame you for crossing the line...

As I trace the potentially delicious print of your lips erupting on mine

Friend and foe...destined frenemy...lover and all

I wish I knew how this would go

But so on...go on

I wander with no attachment...

Let's see where this will flow...

*...But so on...go on*

# Her Lust…The Love

*"…your smile will be the end of me"*

# The lust of a woman

*S*timulation in the sound of his echoing breath…

Rediscovery…cravings propelling the flow in her veins

Her thirst for a man silent like a longing gaze

The paint of her socialized sexuality perfectly tainting the game

No woman can be a desirer

No woman a "wanter"

No woman to yearn the throb of his veins

The feel of his manhood...

The sense of his taste

The texture of his beard that scratches her face when he moans behind her thrusting and pounding hungrily for that high in S.E.X.

No woman to openly declare lest she's labeled Jezebel, the harlot with no shame

It's all hush hush inside my...I mean her chest

His sight increases her heart rate as her woman-parts call for his name

The rise and fall of her breasts signaling a desperate welcome to this glorious man

To pleasure her and succumb to each and every one of her moans

Her want for ecstasy plaguing her body...

The reality of it all shaming that communal "glory"

"Glory" at her required chastity

The status of her crown on a village stool...

The lust of a woman

Both lips...threaded with thick masking tape

Sssssshhhhhhh no word to be spoken...apart from her private bed

*...The lust of a woman*

# This woman loved

*I* want to be loved…the love to feel like the wings of a bird…

I want to be loved…like the wind lightly whispers and blows on my face…

Love me without ownership and I will freely give myself to you…

Submit to a king who rules without a fist but with a love that loves and endures endlessly…

*This woman loved*

I want to be loved by a love that frees me...

That lets me float...with no burden of showing my cracks or weakest points...

I want to be loved like a kiss that caresses...like that kiss that heals a broken wound...just like the kiss a mother gives the bruised knee of the fruit of her womb...

I want to be loved by a man who loves himself for if he does, he will love me more as I'm a part of him...his extension of his heart external to him...rib of his rib...

Flesh of his flesh...

I want to be loved by life itself...

I want to be loved such that I have no question of the heart that loves me...

Imperfect person to love me perfectly...

Your true love will exonerate me...

It will reveal me...

See me and honor me...

So it does to me as it should to you...

Show me how it's done...teach me...

Love me as I learn to love you...

*... This woman loved*

# Parallels

*You*..........

The canvas of my meditations...

Colors contained...portrayed...beautifully exposed...

Set myself free beyond any limitations...

Letting you consume my most intimate thoughts...

I see you look at me with those beautiful eyes

......then the smile......

That smile I can see through distant miles

"...your smile will be the end of me..."

My parallel...yet only in time and distance...

Yet so parallel again in our unanimous cosmic movement...

Sharing a fixed interval in the same mind, same heart

Same thought...complements

Loving you through time...beyond reason

Haunting me of my past wounded love treason

Life mercilessly placing us on parallel streams...

Flowing apart...never to meet

So near, same tendencies, same direction, same tonic

Yet out of reach...way beyond a mountain of a thousand
passionate kisses

Finally together in a perfect parallel universe...

Matching also yet opposing the parallel present...

Gratitude of a past at least shared...

Ghost memories to remember...but not really there...

My parallel...yet only in time and distance...

# Two Magnetic Stones

A wave, a flow...a breeze
　　A current in his touch...time always stands still
In this magnetic second...
　　Stolen moments pass by swiftly like a breeze
Gently yet strongly...
　　　　　Paradoxically sweet...


　A force, a pull...an amazing allure
　　Cosmic synergy unfathomed with an untimely union
　　　Hearts inconceivably vast...their space written in the stars
　　　Their dust affirmed possibly on matching arms

*...Two Magnetic Stones*

# Her wanderings…The search

*The one with a vision*
*Yet, the one disillusioned…*

# Silenced Truth

*So* they say some things
should stay unspoken

Better left unsaid...

Yearning arising for a
release of truth

Though it never promised
to be kind...

Truth never claimed
perfection

Nor did it emotional safety

So my mouth is stifled in silence expected...

Silence adorned...yet silence false...

Silenced truth never to be told...

*...Silenced Truth*

# Own World

*How* did I not know?

Decades of total self-misrepresentation

Voluntary ignorance and self-preserving arrogance

Deceptive mind so mind-blowingly confusing

Judgment impaired, how does one know

How did I not know?

What is there to use as a measure

Apart from statistics in numbers and stature

Does more mean truth?

My truth only but half truth

My perception, my created reality

How did I not know?

I review, disintegrate, seeking all sight

To see me for exactly who I am

Or is that only left for me to label

To stamp and to hold steadfast in my belief

Seeing my own world or does the world see me...

# Heart and Mind

*Organs* from the same entity

Co-relating, functioning rhythmically

Yet they speak different languages

The mind so clear set and sees what society sees

The heart based on flutters of clouded emotion

Vision blurred, it sees only what it wants to see

Each selfish in its function, yet powerful in influence and existence

The obvious oxymoron?

Which is right?

So much commotion and discord

This is not a judgment on either nor is it a choice

Just an observation, a question?

The rest is up to the path of decisions made

*...Heart and Mind*

# Executive Chair

$\mathscr{I}$sold my soul for an executive chair...No...maybe a title...a boss...a company...

All trick masters mirroring an enticing dance...

Freedom I thought...

Freedom to pay my bills...my rent...my fees...the food...alas my pleas kept whispering underneath..."leave"

I ignored...

Fear crippling every liberating thought...

This ain't freedom...it is a soul-sucking vacuum of stress and distress

A hole that gives an illusion of a passage yet has no exit there

I sold my soul the day I sat still and let him strip down my Me

My Me with strengths that even an army of pencils with fat bosoms cannot erase

My education...my work...the fruit of my hands...the mastery of my mind...

My passionate heart...time lost with my daughter brought down to a check

A check I laugh...

One that maybe never came or did when I had to beg

Hovering in my mind now are eminent forces haunting like a tyrant

Realization pulling me from my desperate knees...

Is this what it is?

What it has become?

But what about my Me?!!!

A dollar for my pride…maybe three for my peace…four five six for my voice…selling out piece by piece

This is a light shining on an awareness of the gold-encrusted prison for those who sell out on their dreams…

For a chair…a desk…a boss…a check…

Luring you from your art…taking apart the core of your Me…

# Mistresses

*I* have been a mistress

Don't judge me...

But not to worry

Not YOUR husband's mistress


I have been a mistress

One with a plea

Haunted by shadows

A mistress of my unraveling dreams

I have been a mistress

One plagued with fear

Will they catch me...? Will I? Will she?

Catch herself, catch her dreams

They are whispering longingly between her silky sheets

*Sexy Mountains*

I have been a
mistress

Playing hide
and seek

The mistress
beloved…

Visible yet
invisible to the
kiss…

I have been a mistress

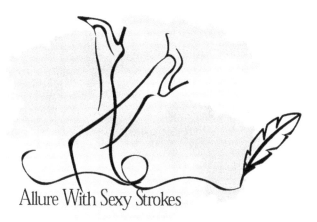

Allure With Sexy Strokes

To strut in my black sexy heels

To dance the dance and learn the art to seduce

To excite...to incite...to allure with sexy strokes

To attract and manifest desires implored

From thought to paper to tangible things...


I have been a mistress...

Drowning in thoughts of gifts of diamonds and pearls...

I've been a mistress


Sexy mountains to be conquered


Foolishly racing and gladly so...

But...let's not forget

The one with a vision

Yet the one disillusioned...

I have been a mistress

A mistress chasing a
shadow of a dream...

*...Mistresses*

# My Face

*If* there is a face that frightens me

It is the face of me

Does it match my thoughts?

Will life meet it all?

Will it be what I dreamt of?

## My Face

The mirror constantly calls my name

Every time I stray from my face

Self-reflection...introspection,

Fearing what that face will say to me

All the betrayal I have stuffed in my cheeks

With endless pain of weeks

Facing myself means facing it all

And coming to terms with me...

If there's a face that frightens me the most

It is the face of me

Will all I believe tend to be true?

Or just a comfort…a sweet cushion to pacify?

My fears about the unknown, things I cannot explain…

Things I cannot predict or predicted with all my might but turned out wrong…

Things that have happened that have not been fair…

The times when reward for wrong exceeded the pain…

My face tells me about the life I've written in the stars

In a world I never did create…

Am I sufficient?

Am I enough?

Can I make it on my own?

Everything else may deceive me

My thoughts...my beliefs...that outside world

But my face...my silent inner being...stays scary and true to me

Is this why I get depressed?

Why I'm so scared of myself

Scared of my limitations and limitlessness...

It's the face I seek, the face I feel

The face that has all the secrets to this

Through it I need to bare it all

The darkness within

The broken kid

The fatherless daughter

The victim of abuse

The cheat

The sweet but weak

The wild horse

The one that does not fit

Mirror mirror on the wall

Who is the scariest of them all?

My reality, my losses, my sins, my shame

My potential, my wins, my glory, my game

It's all on me

And my face points no fingers, it tells on me

...My Face

# Falling

*Feeling* out of touch...

Feeling...falling...floating in a perpetual hole

Fear griping...suffocating...breathe...

Emptiness unspoken

Spinning...rolling...turning...taunting...haunting

Flying maybe...?

Where does suspense go?

Fear, falling, floating…scariest stumble

Succumbing to the hole…

Engulf me whole

Nowhere there…nowhere now

Nowhere but surrender…

Opening my arms...slowly...

Now feeling the fall...the flow

My skin sensates...the heart pulsates...

Taking me to a Destiny unknown...

The Destiny of growth

Facing fears each second of the fall...

Feeling falling floating flowing...

Take me to surrender...here we go

# Her Truth…The discovery

*In the bosom of her private place*
*Is where vacuum became grace…*

# The state of surrender

It floats in the waves

It flows with the motion

It's as light as the whisper

And as silent as the ocean

It roars in the quiet fire

It steals time in space

It's magical in the surrender

As it sparks into your peaceful frame

# Vacuum

*In* that space in which we feel alone

Is the place pregnant with opportunity to be whole

Uncertainty of man is assurance of his soul

Residing in that space...that we end up filling with the known

The drugs...the sex...peer-grown pressure...

Predictable similar tones...

The gossip, the toxins...swimming in the hole

Externalities that crowd the mystery of creation

Your purpose drowning in the need for inclusion...

A vacuum not meant to be filled but felt

In its lone space is magic there...

*Vacuum*

Maybe space is God...

Maybe in that loneliness is where He is shown

Where nothingness becomes nothing less

And in no things you don't become less but more

The mystery of man's limitlessness lay in the comfort of her own loneliness...

In the bosom of her private place

Is where vacuum became grace...

*...Vacuum*

# Acceptance

Acceptance is where alignment lurks

Seeking to return to a place of rest

Where the flow is right

And the "mysteries" ride

Where gratitude is at its best

Acceptance seeks to fulfill

The unfulfilled dreams of the Still

Where the tide hides

Tamed by daylight

Resting on the foundation of the Real

Acceptance is every god's delight

Man accepting the absolute retreat

Realms with all their messes

Splendor and in-between spaces

Just letting it BE as it is...

Perfect world indeed

*...Acceptance*

# Loose woman thou art loosed

In the face of societal scorn

Is where the king-sized bed of freedom to living your truth lies

With voluptuous hips flowing side to side

Unashamed bums jiggling wide

Careless laughter showing all teeth in a loud smile

Hair standing aroused in the slap of a cold breeze

Scorn like rain makes sparkling clean

...A blank slate

This is when the loose woman can be herself

"Loose woman" thou art loosed

From chains of perfection expectancy

Its grips…sinking nails…suffocating you

Now their scorn of unacceptance freeing you

They can finally see you

In the sway of your enticing hips

The blink of your naughty wink

Surely judgment can free you

Loose woman walks through chains like a ghost

When the stones thrown at her can now be used as soles

To step on...glide on...slide on...to move on

*Loose woman thou art loosed*

It's easy for her now you see

For the prison of opinion once tore her

Almost broke her

But now the same fate has freed her

Oh lucky you

Now you can be you

For the worst has already been spoken of you

*Loose woman thou art, loosed*

No longer a slave of public scrutiny

Now just in the realms of your truth and clarity

And only that is gold to you

Loose woman thou art loosed

*...Loose woman, thou art, loosed*

# Her Strength…The tributes

*Because this kind of love is truly why we live*

# I told you

$\mathscr{I}$met a man and I told you

I thought I'd marry him...my friend I told you

I make a mistake I come to you

I'm vulnerable and I feel safe with you

My craziness, my loneliness

All the heartbreaks

You make them less


I drank up and kissed a swine

And I told you

If I danced naked on the vine

I would tell you

My life's stories are written on your palm

My best interests inscribed within your heart

What is life without a true friend I could confide in?

One that listens to me whine and scolds me still when I'm out of line

The best kind is one like wine;

It only gets better with time

Thank you my best one…

Only the angels can match your spine

...I told you

# This is why we live

As the shadow of death whispers

As the devils seek after my soul


As I feel the force of life's vanity

Tired of fighting a battle unknown

As I gasp for hope and faith for meaning and more

As I look into the hollowness within my depths that I run from...


I turn...I turn and I see her face

Sleeping in peaceful surrender and engrossed in sparkly dreams

Gentle heart...sweet soul...

Life-giving, inexplicable love

Greatest teacher of flower bloom

Little Miss Ava...your life holds my purpose and may mine speak words of empowerment into you...

If any other path stays unfulfilled...it's ok...

Because this kind of love is truly why we live

# To My Mother "Bloom"

*Life* sprouts from a burning prairie seed

Seeming doom in the opening of the womb completing the divine deed

Petals like arms...slowly opening in surrender

That wilt in honor to give life to another

Extraordinary beauty...

...In a mother's self sacrifice

Her spirit is like a dandelion

Flying...wandering in wonder

The work of God present...

The work of God art...


If I could name her, I would call her Bloom

# From ashes to dust

As the sound of your voice fades

The core of who you were remains

From ashes to dust...

A sense of the peace you now have settles in my heart...

Feelings of gratitude for the sacrifices you made

For the daughter you took and tried to love as your own

Mountains of challenges we faced

Sometimes you failed, sometimes I did

But the ups and downs have been the foundation of me

The lessons learnt no one can erase

The woman I became

The power of forgiveness I learnt through your death

The best gift you have given me yet

From ashes to dust

The pain will remain

For losing the best man in his imperfections

Was the perfect Dad for me

And Thank You for the guidance you give to me still.

*...From ashes to dust*

# Rivers

As it goes...flows

Torrential river flows...it goes

Stirring through mountains meandering

Its force creating its course

Even in still waters

Calmed down in its plains

Potential energy roars

At times visually gone

Its life...its essence still throbs

Kinda like Wadi Howar vanishing into the Sahara

Just a rainfall away from becoming the Nile again

Rivers synonymous...

To the infinite life in me you create

Different transitional seasons

Nourish my soul...inspire me whole

Fire and passion in me you invigorate

A trickle from a mountain

A drop from a spring

Just One look into my eyes...

And the river begins

... Rivers

# Epilogue

# A Lion's Bow

*This* dream began with a chase

A chase from all the kingdom's best

The kudus...cheetahs, rhinos and even those as tiny as ants

They all seemed to want to a piece of it

Maybe to make a lunch out of me

I ran as fast as the hunted would

Sweat dripping with the tenacity of a survivor's plea

The more I ran the numbers increased

And this quickly chirped at my fighter's will

I slowed...stopped...to face my death at the mercy of the vicious mouths

As I turned to them in surrender I saw their chase not to be a vice

This wasn't a chase of doom

The jungle was exalting me

The king approached with a gigantic roar

I looked straight into the windows of his soul

Those told me all I needed to know

And as I understood the magnitude

The lion bent his majestic knees

And I sighed in gratitude

I stood at a throne as they knelt from row to row

He led the entire troop into a beautiful pattern of a slow magical bow

When I awoke from the dream

The essence of it lingered with me still

That life is never what it seems

Challenges come in disguise with a promise to steal

Yet in reality are there to make you strong as steel

At every turn it may all seem dark and gloomy

But when all has failed and one stops to face and see it for what it is

The awareness lifts you up to a royal walk of fame

All my pain has led me to this gain

Each word created the poems laid on each page


From darkness to dawn

Life's stages are filled with bloom

Never forget even if it's pitch and gloom

Believe, trust, let go

Take it all in

Know that you got this

*...A Lion's Bow*

# Author Profile

Margaret Chideme is a mom to a beautiful 9-year-old girl. She has a blog called Maggie's Diary, where she pours out her thoughts, memories and personal experiences.

She is a poet at heart and loves to indulge in colorful, boundless creative writing as a tool to dive into taboo topics about life, womanhood, ambition and self-discovery. She is passionate about living life with a purpose and venturing into uncharted topics that people shy away from but are important to talk about.

Connect with Margaret Chideme:
Facebook/Instagram: Margaret Chideme the Author
maggiesdiary.com

# What Did You Think of First 30?

*A big thank you for purchasing this book. It means a lot that you chose this book specifically from such a wide range on offer. I do hope you enjoyed it.*

*Book reviews are incredibly important for an author. All feedback helps them improve their writing for future projects and for developing this edition. If you are able to spare a few minutes to post a review on Amazon, that would be much appreciated.*

## Publisher Information

Rowanvale Books provides publishing services to independent authors, writers and poets all over the globe. We deliver a personal, honest and efficient service that allows authors to see their work published, while remaining in control of the process and retaining their creativity. By making publishing services available to authors in a cost-effective and ethical way, we at Rowanvale Books hope to ensure that the local, national and international community benefits from a steady stream of good quality literature.

For more information about us, our authors or our publications, please get in touch.

www.rowanvalebooks.com
info@rowanvalebooks.com

Milton Keynes UK
Ingram Content Group UK Ltd.
UKHW020236221123
432980UK00009B/629

9 781914 422676